Written Tapestries

A collection of Poetry and Prose

by Beckyjean G. Cooke

Written Tapestries
A Collection of Poetry and Prose
by Beckyjean G. Cooke
Published by Indie Artist Press
Eagle Mountain, Utah
www.indieartistpress.com
Second Edition
Copyright © 1985-2014 – All Rights Reserved
ISBN-13: 978-1-62522-013-4
ISBN-10: 1625220138
April, 2015

To my wife and children
for seeing the diamond in the rough;
May I always be worthy of you.

PART ONE 1

My Tree 1
Peaceful Solitude 2
Forward 3
Why? 4

PART TWO 5

Darkness 6
Suicide 8

PART THREE 11

My Muse 13
Conifer Dreams 14
A Day in the Life 15
Return 16
Moments Pause 17
Unpredictable 18
Queen of Fools 19
Mankind's Miracle 20
Passion's Query 21
I Love You 22
Devil or Angel 26
Choices 28
Cannot 29
Dear Richard 30
Waiting 31
You 32
I Am 33
To Be 34
A Break in the Wall 35
Michelle 36
All for the Love of You 37
Lost Talent 38
Something Happened at Work 39
Poetic Ramblings 40
Thank You M'Ladies 43
Obsessed with Melissa 44
Northern Star 45
Excrement 46
Will... 47
What is Ours 48
The Journey 49
The Cycle 50

ONCE MORE	52
IN HER EYES	54
INSPIRED BY BETH	55
REACHING OUT, NOT BACK	57
ABOUT THE POET	**58**

Part One

Beckyjean G. Cooke

A Ninth-Grade English Assignment, a.k.a

My Tree

My favorite tree
      is a weeping willow.
           It stands erect,
     with branches bending low.
The brown of its bark,
      the green of its leaves,
           tell me it thinks there's
     no one it can please.
It sways and it dips,
      when the heavy wind blows;
           leaving no place to settle
     for the tired, black crows.
My tree in the dark
      is a mean, ferocious cat.
           It appears to be frightful
     in the night's deepening black.
I tell you my tree
      reminds myself of me.
           All alone in the world,
     my head bent low,
with my arms resting on my knees.

Peaceful Solitude

High on a hill of lovely green
A picturesque view I've only seen
in dreams.

Flowers bloom around my throne
While birds of song, from the east have flown,
to drink in the stream.

The squirrels that chatter, deer that roam,
Live in peace in my woodland home
away from strife.

My body lies tranquil, my mind at ease.
My soul has gone to a place of peace,
after life.

Beckyjean G. Cooke

Forward

A pool of knowledge
  lays beneath the
      Murky darkness
  of Life's trials,
While light shines
  forth through
eyes once clouded
      by tears.
Peace rests in the
  soft folds of
  a Heart that was
      once Stone,
as Beautiful features
  emerge from clay
    that is molded
      by the hand
        of hardship.

A shoot breaks
  through the ground
as the seed of learning
  receives the nourishment
      of Time,
For Growth always comes
  after the Storm
  has watered the
    Soil;
And a soul that sits
  yearning for
    company,
finds it once
  she stands
and takes a step
      Forward.

Why?

Mind reeling...
Thoughts incoherent...
Fifteen --
Twelve --
Five --
Three --
Who else is there?
Names mean nothing.
Confusion...
Fear...
Anger
Frustration
Are there answers?

Each moment filled with
Uncertainties.
Am I me?

What do you see?
People... Places...
"Why" rings clear
Pain.........
Endless...

How many secrets left?
Who else?
When... Where...

Will I ever know
Peace?

Circles lazily drawn
spiraling down
into... Nothing.

Beckyjean G. Cooke

Part Two

Darkness

Darkness falls heavily over my tortured soul.
The weight of years past crushing the hope of days present.
Viselike tendrils seep into my walls gripping an unguarded heart; Ripping it from a shaky foundation.

Darkness invades, filling the hole once held by my heart. Oozing into every cavern, every crevice, pushing out the remaining sparks of light. Sorrow now rules sending a broken spirit down the tumultuous mountain of Inability.

Darkness sings its own mournful song.
Eerie moans of lost souls join mine in the chorus that is Failure. Reaching with sickly fingers they pull me further into the abyss of Hell. Sirens sing, teeth gnash, sobs form tearless.

There is no Hope. There is no Light. There is Nothing.
☐
☐

Paolo e Francesca by Gustave Doré

Suicide

A tempest rages within.
The swirling waves of loss drowning my will.
The blasting winds of grief silence my cries.

An eternity gone.
A life destroyed.

Oh God let it end!
Let the continued torture
of my existence
cease for those I love!

I run blindly into the street.
Exhausted mentally, spiritually,
physically... I collapse.

Strangely a voice calls,
begging me to rise.
I push it away.
No more. I won't hurt another again!

I will myself to stone,
immovable... unlovable.

Two lights suddenly appear.
The roar of an engine.
The impact sends me flying,
slamming into the ground with bone crunching surety.
□
Again the lights, the roar.
Struck again and tumbled
beneath the vehicle.

Beckyjean G. Cooke

Burning, scrapping the flesh
from my bones as I am dragged
for what seems an eternity.

Finally released I roll to a stop.
Barely conscious I pull myself to safety,
unaware that my arms are broken,
my legs unable to move.

There are people now, surrounding me,
giving aid in attempts to save the life I no longer want.

"Father, please, let me come home!"
Cries every fiber of my being.

Darkness...

Years have passed now.
I've adjusted to being here.
Does He want me?
Not yet, but I'll wait.
Someday I'll get to go home.

Beckyjean G. Cooke

Part Three

My Muse

She speaks.
I listen.
She writes.
I read.
She questions.
I answer.
She hurts.
I bleed.
She looks.
I hide.
She touches.
I reveal.
She warms.
I break.
She holds.
I heal.
She dances.
I sing.
She encourages.
I grow.
She leaves.
I pine.
She loves.
I know.

Conifer Dreams

Mystic miles and Conifer dreams
Rickety styles and crystal streams

Glowing essence Skyward bound
Pearly sheen upon the ground

Midnight flights of Fancy free
Lover lost Come to Me.
☐

Beckyjean G. Cooke

A Day in the Life

Dancing round the house she goes
Washing blankets, dusting throws

Clearing sinks of dirtied dishes
Stops to rest and think on wishes

Rising again, loads to change
In washer, dryer; it's all the same

Never-ending tasks so dreary
Leaving limbs aching and weary

Yet when all is done
She's pleased as punch
With pleasant ladies
She's out to lunch.

Return

Your touch
sends tendrils of comfort
to the hidden wounds
buried
so deep I no longer know
the path to their
healing.

Your kiss
caresses away the fear,
the pain of ages past,
renewing
my resolve and connection
with life.

Your heart
speaks an epic tale
of Love's lost,
Love's search
and Love's finding.

Endless
is the course our souls have traveled.

Timeless
is the connection of our hearts.

They renew
an inner knowledge of each other,
reaffirm their love
and
reward the long absence

Beckyjean G. Cooke

Moments Pause

Fiery tresses drape starlight skin;
Pale and pink blossoms accentuate;
Emerald eyes look not within;
Heaven's smile doth radiate.

Time holds, in awe, its bated breath;
She ponders love's bright horizon;
About her shoulders contentment rests;
Her song of love emblazon.

Eagerly loving, timidly concerned;
She looks towards future happiness;
Many things she hasn't learned;
Pray ye Fates, her course to bless.

Unpredictable

I never know
what will come
out
of this demented
brain
of mine.

What images
my bramble
of
emotions
will illicit.

If
I don't do something
I'll drown.

Beckyjean G. Cooke

Queen of Fools

Storming in my heart,
Lightning in the dark,
Taking down the fences,
Unleashing all my senses.

Touch me so I cry,
My love do not deny,
My every hunger feed,
Your soft caress I need.

Tear down your wall,
Catch me as I fall,
Into your emerald pools,
For I am Queen of fools.

Mankind's Miracle

We seek, we hunt but rarely find,
The blessed miracle of Mankind.
So blind are we of our true worth,
Far from Home we take our search;
Until we lie at death's door,
We needn't look anymore.

Reach out with hands that care for naught,
To grasp and hold the miracle sought.
As others' needs come into view
We'll lose the titles of Me and You.
For truly is there only Us
In the hearts of men who learn to trust.
And with those hands now clean and pure
The love of Man can be assured.

Passion's Query

Whispers echo longing clear
Tendrils weave desires near

Voices form ardent cries
Wingless touch upward flies

Fire's caressing finger burns
Fluid passion savagely churns

Body's quaking limbs unfold
Open heart secrets told

Seeking questions fervently spoken
Answers leaving bond unbroken

I Love You

How
do you tell
someone
you love them?
I've said
and meant
the words a
thousand times over,
but
with each
utterance
I feel
there must be
more.
A better way
to express
vocally
what is only
felt
inwardly.

Hands shake,
heart pounds,
blood flows
as torrential
rains
upon parched
desert.
Warm and cold
simultaneously.
Weak yet stronger
than ever imagined.

How can so much
feeling and
emotion
be shown in
three
little
words?

How
can those words
ever
be enough?

With all
the gifts I
have been given,
with all the
words
I have at
my command,
none
can help
me.
None
can save
me
from this intense
feeling of
inadequacy.

And yet
with each
trickle of
sensation,
I shudder
in other

worldly delight.
Real
becomes fantasy.
Fantasy
becomes real.

A single
touch,
a whispered
word
and a raging
blaze
consumes
my every
thought.
My soul
flies,
my body
dances,
my voice
sings,
my eyes
cry...

All joyfully
for the
love
so freely
given,
so earnestly
felt.
Even my body
cannot find
a single
expression,
how ever

do I
expect
to find a
single word,
a simple
phrase?

They will
never be
enough,
yet
they are
all that
I have.

                    I Love You

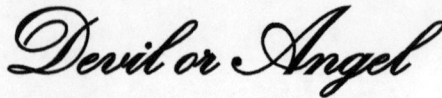

Devils walk
Devils crawl
Devils seep
into my dreams.

Devils scream
Devils talk
Devils sing
into my days.

Devils dive
Devils swim
Devils float
into my mind.

Devils rise
Devils fly
Devils soar
into my soul.

Devils hunger
Devils linger
Devil's finger
crooks in beckoning.

Devil's Call
Devil's laughter
Devil's Daughter
formed in ME.

I Am No More
I Am Nothing

Darkness swirls
Darkness dances
lost forever in the Abyss

No longer Real
No longer feel
lost eternally, never missed.

I Am Deaf
I Am Blind

Piercing shaft
brightness pure
searing chaos' frightening tool

Out of darkness
Out of dread
pulled beyond the gaping maw.

Angels whisper
Angels sing
Angels call
into my dreams

Angels lift
Angels carry
Angels hold
my wounded soul

Angels watch
Angels bless
Angels Dress
ME in Light

Angels comfort
Angels sooth
Angels speak
the purest Truth

                                              Devils deceive... even ME.

Choices

Whatever road we traveling take,
bright horizons our wanderings make;

ever searching twixt light and dark
to find where're we leave our mark.

Our souls combine, to learn anew,
with other voices our changing view;

ever seeing beyond the veil,
we write and speak our different tales.

With each new telling our voices grow
into a chorus of those who know;

ever singing a triumphant song,
"Love your life and live it strong!"

Cannot

Dark and musty, vacant smile;
misconception twisted wild;
friendship pure now bittersweet;
should it be till next we meet...?

Silence needed, a heart rended
hurtful honesty extended.
Can the moment be truly saved?
Is all for naught the love I gave?

Ever open... how can I be
when walls do threaten enclosing me?
Shut down complete, the victr'y won;
voices speak it must be done.

Huddled silent, gagged an' bound,
lofty dreams crash to the ground.
Painful memories of failures past,
I cannot win... I know at last.

Dear Richard

You held me when no one saw me.
You gave me strength when I was too weak to breathe.
You walked with me when others ran away.
You taught me to laugh when my eyes were full of tears.
You gentled my stormy days with a mere smile.
You were my secret friend when I had none.
You made time for me on your way Home,
Saying a gentle goodbye I didn't recognize.
Why me? I'll never know, but I heard you, saw you on your way.

Thanks for that last hug.

Until next we meet...

Waiting

Waiting...

Constantly
waiting for you.

We walk your path,
travel at your pace.
I wander off,
You pull me back.

Searching am I
for the shortcut
to your Confidence.
Which turn
will awaken you
to see me clearly?
To allow me the Hope
of Eternity in your arms,
without Secrets
or Lies?

Will you ever
Love me
More?

Will you ever
find the courage
to be
Free?

My questions go on
as I am still

Waiting...

You

Coming or going
both leave me the same...
wanting more of You.

Push me,
pull me,
twist my thoughts
to your design.

Every command
rapture to my soul,
every moment
engorged with desire.

Brush my mind,
take my heart,
lay me down
to wallow
in supplication,
willingly trusting,
vivaciously hungry
for endless partaking
of You.

I Am

Sensuality grips me in a bold embrace
Passion clings to me, there is no escape

Wants yearning
Needs burning
Hunger screams its desire for You.

Every touch lingers on my skin
Every kiss crawls deeper within

Hands tremble
Walls crumble
Eagerly my heart reaches for You.

Spirituality soars along astral skies
Sexuality engulfs me, no more lies

Hearts undying
Souls uniting
I am Here; I am There; I am You.

To Be

Tease the Essence of the Soul
Torture the Passions of Lust
Temper the Vanity raging
Trust the Heart holding You

Observe the Patterns of Love
Open the Mind to their Weaving
Onward the Courageous falcon flies
Over the Barren landscape of Hope

Bend the Will to Your command
Brush the Strands of Time away
Beckon the Whispering songs to play
Bind the Music to your Life

Embrace the Joy of Wonder
Engage the Constellations above
Enrapture the Child within
Encourage the Future to Prove

Beckyjean G. Cooke

A Break in the Wall

I want to cry.
I want to scream.
I need to hide
in you...

But you're not there.

Your own life has made demands on you,
taken so much of you from me.
You try to let me know
I'm still thought of...

Somewhere in your chaos.

Once upon a time,
I used to have
so much of you,
now I'm a dog...

Begging for scraps.

I feel as if walls
are closing in on me.
Yet your love encircles,
entwining, binding...

My soul to you.

Forever will I wait for you
to return wholly to me.
This is just a breach
in my wall of patience.

I love you.

Michelle

"You were always my best supporter."
Written on the back of a photograph.
Twenty years later, read again,
the words held new meaning.

Today I see a new friend
blossom from within the old.
An offering given freely,
never retracted.
One regret looms:
Why didn't I see it sooner?

All the time wasted.
All the words never shared.
All the memories never made.
All the world faded...

Another chance, a new life.
Will this morning bring a soaring tale,
an enlightened song?
Fate, do not let this one pass.

All for the Love of You

Like a summer wind warms the earth,
your love tenderly caresses my being,
gently combing through my hair,
dancing down my arms,
kissing my neck with each tender pass.

The symphony of You
reverberates in the timbre of your voice
as you speak of your days with the boys,
their mishaps,
their joys,
the adventures,
the tragedies
musically enraptures my heart,
cascading over my soul.

Blissfully I enter my dreams,
joyously I greet the dawn,
each day brings me You,
each day grows more tender,
more pregnant with shining moments
of clarity,
anticipation,
and wonder.

Look what You have gifted me,
see the colors You have painted upon my canvas,
feel the tremors of the quickening in my soul,
hear the thunderous chorus ringing in my words...
all for the love of YOU.

Lost Talent

"An angel's voice", "dulcet tones drifting
airy in cadence, strong in rhythm"
"We Love You" they said true
"Sing for us", they shouted "More"
It fell on deaf ears

Each wave of accolades drowned desire
Each toss of coin burned fire

A cold winter, an evil cough
harsh scratches echo, gravel grinds gritty
Ears turn from the dank sound
"No More" they wearily cry out
"The pain is too great"

If she'd only loved, only knew
What others craved, vowed true

She wallows in dark self pity
her gift stolen in a season
No more will they gather round
The damage has been completely done
Ne'er again will she sing

Fear not your talents to share
Embrace them, nurture them with care

You may never know when, where
they will leave you, taken away;
Treasure what you have, share it
only when shared will they grow
Never, ever, be like me.

Something Happened at Work

Tension runs wildly
through the ranks.
Indicators of shame
blister their skin.
Blame vacillates incessantly
leaving gaping wounds.
Fortitude rises calmly
wrapping all concerned.
Confidence beams radiantly
healing tender scars.

Poetic Ramblings

Rambling One
Forever marks the turning of chaos
into ethereal strands weaving back
and forth through time,
bending the mind,
taming the soul;
creating ordered Reality
only to collapse upon itself
in a single moment.

Rambling Two
Touch the rays of Hope
as they encircle the world.
Reach out and grasp
the fleeting wisps of Charity
flying forth to galaxies unknown.
Chase the dreams running toward the stars,
disappearing into the Void.
Try and capture Innocence as it hides
beneath the roiling surface of a distant nova.

Rambling Three
Tender moments cut more
deeply across the Soul
than swords upon skin,
yet they leave no trail,
no stain of Crimson life
but a rainbow of emotions
like cool fire dancing
across the expanse of
Mortality.

Rambling Four
Emotional fires in cyclonic pillars
tear through my existence
leaving smoldering rubble
in their wake.
Time extends and collapses
upon itself wearing down the mind
until nothing is real.
Struggling, climbing, running
for the freedom that eludes capture,
destroying the hope I so desperately cling to.
Step into the abyss,
let it swallow me whole
as I embrace the oblivion offered...
if only for a moment

Rambling Five
Rainbow ribbons rustle the wind,
harnessing the energy
bleeding into the night.
Touch the tender lights of love,
flickering forth from hearts
careworn and weary.
Life batters them to and fro
but still they burn brighter,
seeking each other
in a swirling mist of uncertainty.

Rambling Six
Stars kiss the night sky like jewels upon velvet.
Wispy clouds trail forth adding to the shimmer.
The sliver of moon gives off her pale light in counterpoint.
Silhouettes of trees, their eerie arms reaching out for naught
but life, step into the world of twilight to embrace ethereal
beings in their darkened walks.

The wind, oh the wind, dances about souls who linger,
creeping into hair, eyes, ears, between toes and fingers as each
passes upon a course only they know.

Stop a moment in your sojourn.

Let the breath of life encompass you, caress you,
love you in a way nothing else can.

Feel the tiny hairs upon your skin rise in greeting,
begging to be touched by the unseen.

Let your eyes burn with dryness as you fight to keep them
open, seeing the richness of the night until they water,
creating rivulets upon your chilled cheeks.

Open your soul to the beckoning of spirits that writhe beside
you, carrying you upon astral planes to envision wonders and
mysteries your conscious will soon forget but your heart will
remember.

Feel the earth beneath your feet as you gently descend,
laying within its embrace to view in greater expanse the
heavens above.

Stare long and hard until you can reach up and touch each
star, trail your fingers through each cloud feeling the dew
suckle your skin as the wind lays upon you,
blanketing you as slumber steels your mind.

Let go.

Just Let Go.

Thank You M'Ladies

Timeless questions weave indecision through her veins.
A hunger grips her, an old adversary, resurfacing to begin anew the battle within her heart.

Searching, drifting on the tides of cyberspace then washed ashore upon an island of creativity, of emotions thick and roiling, pulling at her stronger than the waves attempting to suck her back under. She climbs timidly, slowly to her feet looking about her in wonder.

Each spark of light floating before her, leading her hither and yon, calling upon her essence to join them as one by one they dance, their individuality shimmering in every hue of desire. Her own light inconsistently flickers hot than cool until one light, seemingly aloof from the others, comes near enough to caress with its warmth.

A chance encounter drowning her senses as she unwittingly follows, learning from each cadence of its mercurial dance. This light, oh so feminine in the way it moves, strong, confident, determined, while soft and compassionate, becomes her professor of the heart, teaching her to open herself to the inner light beckoning, pleading for release.

The Muse engulfs her, stripping away the ancient layers, lowering the veil that has kept her hidden from introspection.
An explosion of greens, reds, and blues follows.
Now free, she floats and dances with her sister lights upon their island in the universe, content, at peace…

Home.

Obsessed with Melissa

If only my fingers could type in time with the music playing dearest to my heart. The poetry dripping from your lips as your fingers caress a symphony of emotions elicited from the guitar you hold closer than your lover. Philosophy, theology, social commentaries: all have their place within your words, your songs; each forming a united front against the cruelties evident in the world. And yet you manage to wrap them tenderly in a cocoon of melodies, harmonies and lyrics, reaching out to needy hearts like tendrils of omniscience, somehow knowing the individual better than themselves. I close my eyes and entertain fantasy; you knowing me, caressing me, loving me from the safety of a recording studio. The letter you've written through the guise of song titles, I know well…

"(How Would I Know) (If I Wanted To)?
(Will You Still Love Me) (When You Find The One)?
(Come Out Tonight).
(Kiss Me) (All The Way To Heaven).
(I'm The Only One) (This Moment).
(Please Forgive Me), (Heal Me).
(I Want To Be In Love).

(Watching You) (Come To My Window), (I Will Never Be The Same).
(The Late September Dogs) (Occasionally) (Breathe) (Mercy).
(Tuesday Morning), (Meet Me In The Dark) (If You Want To).

(Enough Of Me) (My Lover).
(Sleep).

(Your Little Secret)"

The fantasy, the dreams tightly entwine with the music. Obsession is my home, my only desire, my only course. But then you were always (Stronger Than Me).

Beckyjean G. Cooke

Northern Star

A tribute to Melanie Jayne Chisholm

One in a crowd
hiding well
the silent yearning clear
the voice of an angel
the spirit from hell
turning the world on her ear

You felt the rock
you danced the roll
amid cheers and jeers
You swam the sea
you paid the toll
and cried the joyful tears

A heart of light
a burning fire
within the mainstream fare
you took control
flying higher
to reach what few will dare

Your standard dances
above the stars
celestial glories call
the fight is over
the wounds are scars
rewarded you stand tall

Excrement

What is wrong with me?
Why am I awake?
Am I awake?
No.
This is a dream.
All of life is a dream.
Reality never fully plays.

Each breath exists only to tease;
To permeate the mind,
Convincing it.
Deception.
Winding forward.
Twisting back upon itself.
Until nothing is real or false.

The senses create, coalescing cosmic goo
Into tangible beliefs, dancing
For our entertainment.
Excrement.
Wipe it clean
From your boots, your hands.
Grasp Nothing, for that is all Existence.

Will the years continue to be kind
Will the mind know the passing of years
Will forever come in a day
Will that day spill out an eternity
Will I live each moment for others
Will another give me a moment to live
Will I love until I die
Will I ever die for love
Will my questions find an answer
Will the answers become more questions

When you hold the moment
You hold Eternity

What is Ours

Let us not forget our true desires;
light the match, start the fires
enter into life's eternal flame
let it scorch, twist, and rename
our souls.

Minds churning,
hearts burning, hands yearning
to take what is given
to touch ANY heaven
that breathes upon this earth,
tasting Life with each rebirth
of passion.

Fevered screams
raging through the dreams,
of each traveler amongst the stars
in constant wonder of what is ours
to give.

The Journey

Time travels fast
look ahead, not past.
Follow the Road at hand:
Take every fork, every Bend.
Never turn from
Journeys won.

Happy souls Dance
when Harmonies chance
a meeting with Heart;
Take the path, be a part
of Life. Try the world -
Make It Sure.

The Cycle

Words of the past
echo blaringly
cover my ears,
cover my heart
emotions strangle
the surety hard won
the cycle repeats,
ever circling
about my soul.

Tying,
binding
inner wings
flight grounded
voice hushed
sight blinded

Words of the present
sing softly
touch my ears,
touch my heart
feelings uplift
the spirit thought crushed
the cycle continues,
ever calling
my soul to rise.

Floating,
soaring
with inner wings
flight returns
voice sings

Beckyjean G. Cooke

sight pure

Hopes of the future
call enticingly
free my mind
free my heart
possibilities expand
the sphere of existence
the cycle moves on
ever turning
my soul around.

Walking,
running
with folded wings
flight optional
voice quiet
sight eternal

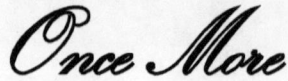

Once More

Once more...

twisting in the wind
roots untangle from earth
knock me over
drive me down

Once more...

words honestly spoken sear
a heart drowns anew
tie me up
leave me bleeding

Once more...

what's dead is reborn
what's buried crawls through
let it free
let it breathe

Once more...

scream love in anger
cry happiness in hate
embrace the void
clip my wings

Once more...

I hear your song
You tease my mind

caress my soul
kiss my wounds

Once more...

trust trembles to hold
love hungers to feed
beat them away
break their spirit

Once more...

turning away the truth
burning away the hope
never give up
never give in

Once more... Never

In Her Eyes

upward fly
downward slide
racing faster
dying sooner

ending life without a care
leaving others whimpering still
never looking behind or sideways
only looking toward the next sunset

hiding in the twilight hours
buried 'neath pure white flowers
ever silent now you'll be
taken by yourself from me

how will i live this life alone
how will i carry this heavy load

time stands still
the screaming done
i look and see
I AM The One

lying silent cold and broken
upon the dreary blacktop road
your cries are muted
my ears fill with blood
I never knew I was so loved.

Inspired by Beth

Filled with dread, remorse and pain
I read your words, she feels the same
Forever denied my desired destiny
in her arms where I'd be free
but life dealt me the strangest hand
I failed to see, to understand
her turmoil within, the scope of sin
she held too long the past that's been
her burden true, her guilty crime
held like a lover lost in time
she breathes the dirt, tastes the air
I wish for once she'd stay right here
and hold on tight, never fearing the love
I ache to share, I long to prove
I am here forever should she only see
I now know she never truly belonged to me.

A higher being is her one goal
To soar the stars to dance the shoals
she slumbers deep her caresses bear
the gift of deceit to her own love's care
she never saw the glory that shown
about her soul until a love lost known
I truly pray she knows the song
that I sing for her now that she's gone
I truly hope she one day hears
the chorus I sing, the applause I cheer
for her own growth away from me
I am a cancer the blackest disease
Cut me out, eradicate the memories
Leave them to fry in unholy grease
cast aside the fraudulent joys

break them soundly like rotting toys.

I should travel alone this wandering road
yet I must Need to share another's load
there is one who has stood all along,
by me, never wavering, supporting strong
my every decision that brought her pain
she never sought more than she'd gain
from this fractured soul I enshroud within
hiding from the world my deepest sin
I pray now that I will never keep
another soul in this watery deep
of my travails, my sickly fingers
no longer entangle, will no longer linger
upon the fragile thoughts of what could be
I seek no more my fantasy
I am content with what God has given
I live this life each moment Heaven.

Reaching Out Not Back

The person I was is so much a stranger to me now.
Reading the past to feel who She was.
Confusion, darkness warring constantly with Light.

There is no desire to resurrect a past of pain.
Determined to once and for all move forward.
Stepping closer towards a brighter future.

Leave her in her grave.

About the Poet

Beckyjean G. Cooke is a wife and mother of somewhere between four and nine or ten biological, step and elected children. She is also a grandmother, known affectionately as "Poppy" to at least six amazing children, although she and her wife do tend to lose count.

She enjoys reading, writing and avoiding both through endless pursuits of online poker, farming and laundry. She makes her home in Utah with her wife and children.

Beckyjean G. Cooke

Other Books from Indie Artist Press

A Rancher's Woman by E Ayers
Witch by Rebecca Little
Dance In My Heart by Marjorie Jones
Hunting Camion by Raleigh Kincaid
Loving the Heartland by Marjorie Jones

Coming in 2015

With This Ring by E. Ayers
I Thee Wed by E. Ayers
To Have & To Hold by E. Ayers
Firelight by Starla Childs
A Rancher's Dream by E. Ayers

Non-Fiction:
Simply Successful by Evan W. Dorren

Witch by Rebecca Little

Find these titles and more on our website at
http://www.indieartispress.com

www.ingramcontent.com/pod-product-compliance
Lightning Source LLC
Chambersburg PA
CBHW060506080526
44584CB00015B/1569